Solar System Explorers

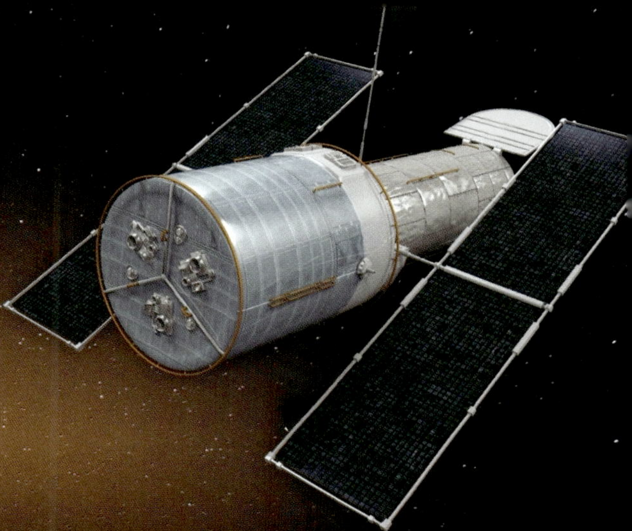

Saturn

Written by Rebekah Banks

KidHaven Publishing

Published in 2026 by
KidHaven Publishing, an Imprint of
Greenhaven Publishing, LLC
2544 Clinton St., Buffalo, NY 14224

Written by: Rebekah Banks
Edited by: Noah Leatherland
Designed by: Amelia Harris

Cataloging-in-Publication Data
Names: Banks, Rebekah.
Title: Saturn / Rebekah Banks.
Description: Buffalo, NY : Kidhaven Publishing, 2026. | Series: Solar System Explorers | Includes glossary and index
Identifiers: ISBN 9781534549883 (pbk) | ISBN 9781534549890 (library bound) | ISBN 9781534549906 (ebook)
Subjects: LCSH: Saturn (Planet)—Juvenile Literature
Classification: LCC QB671 B36 2026 | DDC 523.48--dc25

Manufactured in the United States of America

CPSIA compliance information: Batch #CSKH26
For further information contact Greenhaven Publishing LLC at 1-844-317-7404.

Please visit our website, www.greenhavenpublishing.com.
For a free color catalog of all our high-quality books, call toll free 1-844-317-7404 or fax 1-844-317-7405.

Find us on

Image Credits

Images are courtesy of Shutterstock.com. With thanks to Getty Images, Thinkstock Photo and iStockphoto. Cover – AspctStyle, andreysharonov, aappp, 19 STUDIO. Recurring Images – thomas eder, YummyBuum, Sabelskaya. 4–5 – Nsit, Joseph Jacobs. 6–7 – bilgeari, Triff. 8–9 – NASA images, joshimerbin. 10–11 – AspctStyle. 12–13 – Vadim Sadovski, Artsiom P. 14–15 – Mikael Damkier, Pike-28, Vlad Ra27. 16–17 – Antony McAulay, david.costa.art. 18–19 – Andrei Armiagov, BreizhAtao. 20–21 – Claudio Caridi. 22–23 – Amanda Carden, Nsit.

Contents

Words that look like **this** can be found in the glossary on page 24.

Let's Explore!

Have you ever imagined what life is like in space? Let's find out as we explore our solar system. We will tell you all you need to know about the planets around the sun!

The solar system is made up of eight planets and five dwarf planets that **orbit** the sun. Exploring all the planets is a difficult job, but we are here to help you!

Where Is Saturn?

All planets in the solar system orbit the sun at different distances. If we were looking at them lined up, they would look like this:

Saturn is the sixth planet from the sun. It is between Jupiter and Uranus. Saturn is over 886 million miles (1.4 billion km) from the sun. Can you spot the large rings around Saturn?

Round and Round

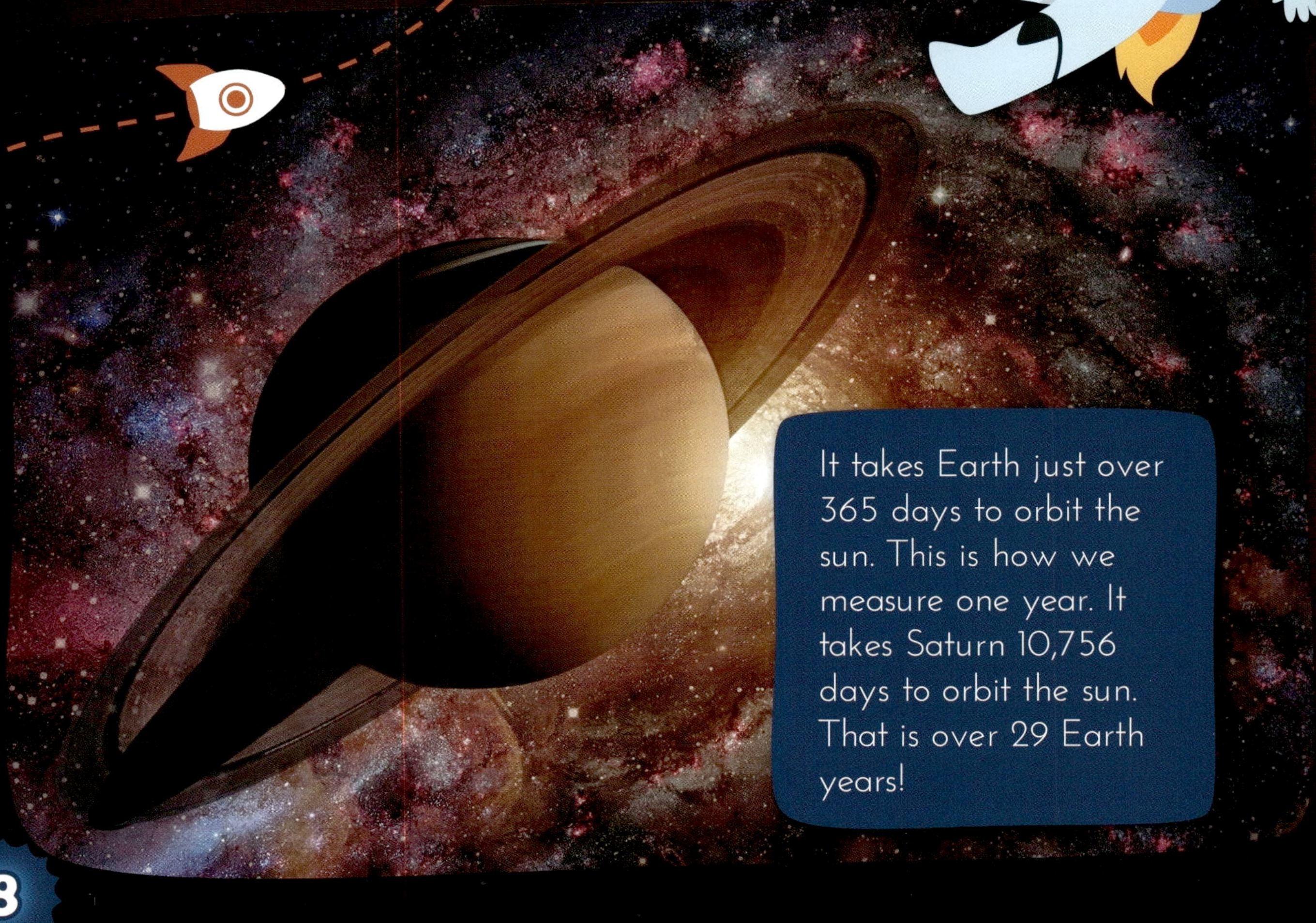

It takes Earth just over 365 days to orbit the sun. This is how we measure one year. It takes Saturn 10,756 days to orbit the sun. That is over 29 Earth years!

As Saturn orbits the sun, it spins on an **axis**. A day on Saturn is just over 10 hours long. That is the second shortest day in the solar system.

Planet Profile

Here are some notes on Saturn from our database.

Temperature

Saturn is around minus 220 degrees Fahrenheit (-140°C).

Size

- Around: 235,298 miles (378,675 km)
- Across: 74,897 miles (120,500 km)

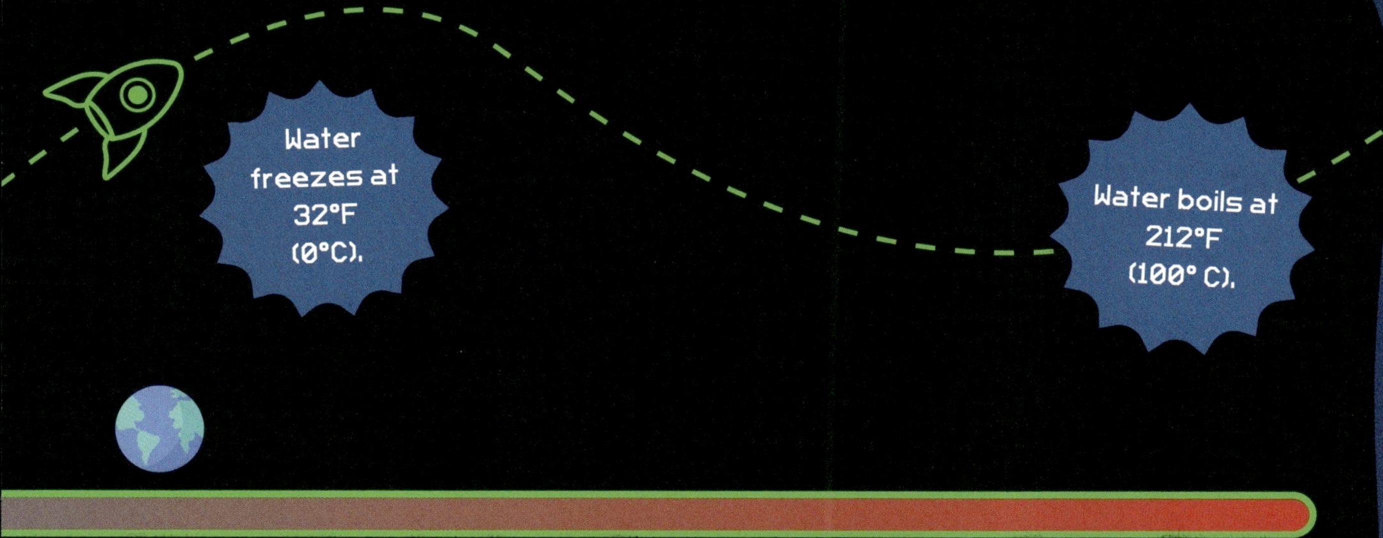

What Is Saturn Made Of?

Saturn is a planet made up of swirling **gas** and **liquid**. It is a type of planet called a gas giant. The main gases that make up Saturn are called hydrogen and helium.

Saturn is thought to have a few different layers.

Atmosphere

Saturn's **atmosphere** is made of different gases.

Liquid and Gas

Below Saturn's atmosphere, there are layers of liquid and gas.

Core

Saturn's center is made of metal and rock.

Watching the Weather

Saturn is a very cloudy place. From our spaceship, you can see wavy white patterns. These patterns are huge storms. The wind on Saturn is around five times stronger than the wind on Earth!

There is something that looks like a hexagon at the top of Saturn. The hexagon is a wavy jet stream of winds with a giant storm in the middle. Nowhere else in the solar system has weather like this.

Is There Life on Saturn?

Saturn is a gas giant. Gas giants do not have a **surface**. This means there is no land or water. No living thing would be able to **survive** there.

Saturn may not be habitable, but one of its moons could be. The moon Titan has a thick atmosphere and an ocean of water. One day, it may be able to support life.

Spot the Satellites

Something that orbits a larger object in space is called a satellite. A moon is a **natural** satellite. Humans have also made satellites and sent them into space. They are used to research things in space.

Saturn has 146 known moons. Some moons are as big as a planet. Some are as small as a football field. Saturn's largest moons are called Titan, Rhea, and Iapetus.

Rocky Rings

Saturn is famous for its rings. These huge rings are made up of lots of pieces of ice and rock. The rings orbit Saturn like a satellite.

Some pieces that make up Saturn's rings are as small as a grain of sand. Others are as large as a mountain. The five rings move at different speeds, which makes them look like one giant circle.

Take a closer look at Saturn's rings.

More to Explore

What a super time we have had on Saturn! We have learned so many things about this gas giant and its huge rings. What is your favorite fact about Saturn?

For now, it is time to wave goodbye to Saturn. As we continue our mission, we will explore even more planets. There are so many places left to explore!

Glossary

atmosphere the mixture of gases that makes up the air and surroundings

axis an imaginary line that something turns on

degrees measuring units used to explain how hot or cold something is

gas a thing that is like air, which spreads out to fill any space available

liquid a material that flows, such as water

natural found in nature and not made by people

orbit move around a star or planet in a curved path

surface the outside layer of something

survive to stay alive

Index

Solar System Explorers

Mercury

Charis Mather

Solar System Explorers

Titles in This Series

- Earth
- Jupiter
- Mars
- Mercury
- Neptune
- Pluto and Other Dwarf Planets
- Saturn
- Uranus
- Venus

KidHaven
PUBLISHING

ISBN: 9781534549883
9 781534 549883